50 Hawaiian Fusion Recipes for Home

By: Kelly Johnson

Table of Contents

- Grilled Pineapple with Honey Lime Glaze
- Coconut Shrimp
- Mango Salsa
- Macadamia nuts
- Taro
- Spam
- Poke
- Lomi-lomi salmon
- Kalua pork
- Poi
- Shoyu
- Guava
- Lilikoi (passion fruit)
- Huli-huli chicken
- Haupia (coconut pudding)
- Lau Lau
- Mahi mahi
- Ahi tuna
- Ono (wahoo fish)
- Huli-huli sauce
- Teriyaki
- Teriyaki-glazed
- Teriyaki chicken
- Teriyaki beef
- Teriyaki salmon
- Huli-huli pineapple
- Huli-huli sauce
- Grilled pineapple
- Coconut shrimp
- Coconut chicken
- Loco moco
- Musubi
- Hawaiian roll
- Hawaiian barbecue
- Kona coffee

- Kona blend
- Kona coffee rub
- Kalbi ribs
- Pineapple salsa
- Mango salsa
- Pineapple coleslaw
- Taro chips
- Macadamia crusted
- Macadamia nut dressing
- Macadamia nut pie
- Haupia pie
- Haupia cake
- Lava flow cocktail
- Mai Tai
- Hawaiian sunset cocktail

Grilled Pineapple with Honey Lime Glaze

Ingredients:

- 1 pineapple, peeled, cored, and cut into slices
- 1/4 cup honey
- 2 tablespoons lime juice
- 1 teaspoon lime zest
- Pinch of salt
- Fresh mint leaves, for garnish (optional)

Instructions:

1. Preheat your grill to medium-high heat.
2. In a small bowl, whisk together the honey, lime juice, lime zest, and a pinch of salt until well combined.
3. Brush both sides of the pineapple slices with the honey lime glaze.
4. Place the pineapple slices on the preheated grill and cook for 3-4 minutes per side, or until grill marks form and the pineapple is slightly caramelized.
5. Remove the grilled pineapple slices from the grill and transfer them to a serving platter.
6. Drizzle any remaining honey lime glaze over the grilled pineapple slices.
7. Garnish with fresh mint leaves, if desired.
8. Serve the grilled pineapple warm as a side dish, dessert, or as a topping for grilled meats or salads.

Enjoy the sweet and tangy flavor of the grilled pineapple with the refreshing touch of lime and honey!

Coconut Shrimp

Ingredients:

- 1 pound large shrimp, peeled and deveined
- 1 cup shredded coconut (sweetened or unsweetened, depending on preference)
- 1 cup panko breadcrumbs
- 2 eggs, beaten
- 1/2 cup all-purpose flour
- Salt and pepper to taste
- Oil for frying

For the dipping sauce:

- 1/4 cup sweet chili sauce
- 2 tablespoons mayonnaise
- 1 tablespoon lime juice
- 1 teaspoon soy sauce

Instructions:

1. Preheat your oven to 375°F (190°C). Line a baking sheet with parchment paper.
2. Set up a breading station with three shallow bowls. In one bowl, place the flour. In the second bowl, beat the eggs. In the third bowl, combine the shredded coconut and panko breadcrumbs.
3. Season the shrimp with salt and pepper. Working one at a time, dredge each shrimp in the flour, shaking off any excess. Then dip it into the beaten egg, allowing any excess to drip off. Finally, coat the shrimp in the coconut breadcrumb mixture, pressing gently to adhere.
4. Place the coated shrimp onto the prepared baking sheet. Repeat with the remaining shrimp.
5. Once all the shrimp are coated, spray them lightly with cooking spray or drizzle with olive oil. This will help them brown nicely in the oven.
6. Bake the shrimp in the preheated oven for 12-15 minutes, or until the coconut is golden brown and the shrimp are cooked through, flipping halfway through.
7. While the shrimp are baking, prepare the dipping sauce by whisking together the sweet chili sauce, mayonnaise, lime juice, and soy sauce in a small bowl.

8. Once the shrimp are done, remove them from the oven and let them cool for a few minutes before serving.
9. Serve the coconut shrimp with the dipping sauce on the side.

Enjoy your crispy and delicious Coconut Shrimp!

Mango Salsa

Ingredients:

- 2 ripe mangoes, peeled, pitted, and diced
- 1/2 red onion, finely chopped
- 1 red bell pepper, diced
- 1 jalapeño pepper, seeded and minced
- 1/4 cup fresh cilantro, chopped
- Juice of 1 lime
- Salt and pepper to taste

Instructions:

1. In a large bowl, combine the diced mangoes, chopped red onion, diced red bell pepper, minced jalapeño pepper, and chopped cilantro.
2. Squeeze the lime juice over the mango mixture and toss gently to combine.
3. Season the salsa with salt and pepper to taste, adjusting the seasoning as needed.
4. Cover the bowl and refrigerate the mango salsa for at least 30 minutes to allow the flavors to meld together.
5. Once chilled, give the salsa a final stir and taste test before serving.
6. Serve the mango salsa as a topping for grilled fish, chicken, tacos, or alongside tortilla chips for dipping.

This mango salsa is bursting with flavor and makes a perfect accompaniment to any dish, adding a tropical and refreshing twist to your meals. Enjoy!

Macadamia nuts

Ingredients:

- 4 Mahi Mahi fillets
- 1 cup macadamia nuts, finely chopped
- 1/4 cup panko breadcrumbs
- 2 tablespoons fresh parsley, chopped
- 1/4 cup all-purpose flour
- 2 eggs, beaten
- Salt and pepper to taste
- Olive oil for frying

Instructions:

1. Preheat your oven to 375°F (190°C). Line a baking sheet with parchment paper.
2. In a shallow bowl, combine the chopped macadamia nuts, panko breadcrumbs, and chopped parsley. Season with salt and pepper to taste.
3. Place the all-purpose flour in another shallow bowl, and the beaten eggs in a third shallow bowl.
4. Season the Mahi Mahi fillets with salt and pepper.
5. Dredge each fillet in the flour, shaking off any excess. Then dip it into the beaten eggs, allowing any excess to drip off. Finally, coat the fillets in the macadamia nut mixture, pressing gently to adhere.
6. Heat a few tablespoons of olive oil in a large oven-safe skillet over medium-high heat. Once hot, add the Mahi Mahi fillets to the skillet and cook for 2-3 minutes on each side until golden brown.
7. Transfer the skillet to the preheated oven and bake for an additional 10-12 minutes, or until the Mahi Mahi is cooked through and flakes easily with a fork.
8. Remove the skillet from the oven and let the Mahi Mahi rest for a few minutes before serving.
9. Serve the Macadamia Nut Crusted Mahi Mahi with your favorite side dishes and enjoy!

This dish is sure to impress with its crunchy macadamia nut crust and tender Mahi Mahi. It's perfect for a special dinner or anytime you want to elevate your meal with a touch of tropical flavor!

Taro

Ingredients:

- 2 large taro roots
- Vegetable oil for frying
- Salt to taste

Instructions:

1. Peel the taro roots and slice them thinly using a mandoline slicer or a sharp knife. Aim for uniform slices to ensure even cooking.
2. Place the taro slices in a bowl of cold water and let them soak for about 30 minutes. This helps remove excess starch and makes the chips crispier.
3. Drain the taro slices and pat them dry with paper towels to remove any excess moisture.
4. Heat vegetable oil in a deep fryer or large pot to 350°F (175°C).
5. Working in batches, carefully add the taro slices to the hot oil, making sure not to overcrowd the fryer. Fry for 3-4 minutes, or until the chips are golden brown and crispy.
6. Use a slotted spoon or tongs to transfer the fried taro chips to a plate lined with paper towels to drain excess oil.
7. Sprinkle the hot chips with salt to taste while they are still warm.
8. Allow the taro chips to cool completely before serving. Store any leftover chips in an airtight container to maintain their crispiness.

These homemade taro chips make a delicious and addictive snack that's perfect for munching on anytime. Enjoy the unique flavor and crispy texture of these delightful chips!

Spam

Ingredients:

- 1 can of Spam
- 2 cups sushi rice
- 2 1/2 cups water
- 1/4 cup soy sauce
- 2 tablespoons sugar
- 5 sheets nori seaweed
- Furikake seasoning (optional)
- Bamboo sushi mat (optional)

Instructions:

1. Start by cooking the sushi rice. Rinse the rice under cold water until the water runs clear. Then, combine the rice and water in a rice cooker or pot and cook according to the package instructions.
2. While the rice is cooking, prepare the Spam. Cut the Spam into slices about 1/4 inch thick. In a skillet over medium heat, fry the Spam slices until they are golden brown and crispy on each side, about 2-3 minutes per side. Remove from the skillet and set aside.
3. In a small saucepan, combine the soy sauce and sugar. Heat over low heat until the sugar is dissolved, stirring occasionally. Remove from heat and set aside.
4. Once the rice is cooked, fluff it with a fork and let it cool slightly.
5. Lay a sheet of nori seaweed on a clean work surface. Place a spam slice on top of the nori.
6. Wet your hands with water to prevent the rice from sticking, then scoop a small amount of rice and press it firmly onto the Spam slice, forming a layer of rice about 1/2 inch thick.
7. Drizzle a little of the soy sauce mixture over the rice, then sprinkle with furikake seasoning, if desired.
8. Fold the bottom edge of the nori over the rice and Spam, then roll it up tightly, using a bamboo sushi mat if you have one.
9. Use a sharp knife to slice the Spam musubi into individual pieces.
10. Repeat the process with the remaining Spam slices, rice, and nori sheets.

11. Serve the Spam musubi immediately or wrap them individually in plastic wrap for later.

Enjoy your homemade Spam musubi as a tasty snack or lunch option with a Hawaiian twist!

Poke

Ingredients:

- 1 lb sushi-grade ahi tuna, cubed
- 1/4 cup soy sauce
- 1 tablespoon sesame oil
- 1 tablespoon rice vinegar
- 1 teaspoon sriracha sauce (optional)
- 1 teaspoon grated fresh ginger
- 2 green onions, thinly sliced
- 1 teaspoon sesame seeds
- 1 avocado, diced
- 1/4 cup chopped cucumber
- Cooked rice or salad greens, for serving
- Additional toppings: sliced radishes, edamame, seaweed salad, etc. (optional)

Instructions:

1. In a large bowl, whisk together the soy sauce, sesame oil, rice vinegar, sriracha (if using), and grated ginger.
2. Add the cubed ahi tuna to the bowl and gently toss to coat it in the marinade. Cover the bowl and refrigerate for at least 15-30 minutes to allow the flavors to meld together.
3. While the tuna is marinating, prepare any additional toppings you'd like to serve with the poke.
4. Once the tuna has marinated, remove it from the refrigerator and add the sliced green onions, sesame seeds, diced avocado, and chopped cucumber to the bowl. Gently toss everything together until evenly combined.
5. To serve, divide the poke mixture among bowls lined with cooked rice or salad greens. Top with any additional toppings you desire.
6. Enjoy your Ahi Tuna Poke immediately as a delicious and refreshing appetizer or main dish!

Feel free to customize this recipe to suit your taste preferences by adding or omitting ingredients as desired. Enjoy!

Lomi-lomi salmon

Ingredients:

- 1 lb fresh salmon fillet, skin removed
- 2 ripe tomatoes, diced
- 1 small onion, finely chopped
- 2 green onions, thinly sliced
- 1/2 cup diced cucumber
- 1/4 cup chopped cilantro or parsley
- Juice of 1-2 limes
- Salt, to taste
- Optional: chili peppers or jalapeños, seeded and diced for heat (adjust to taste)

Instructions:

1. Rinse the salmon fillet under cold water and pat it dry with paper towels. Cut the salmon into small cubes and place them in a large bowl.
2. Add the diced tomatoes, chopped onion, sliced green onions, diced cucumber, and chopped cilantro or parsley to the bowl with the salmon.
3. Squeeze the lime juice over the mixture and season with salt to taste. If you like it spicy, add diced chili peppers or jalapeños at this point.
4. Gently toss all the ingredients together until well combined. Be careful not to break up the salmon too much.
5. Cover the bowl with plastic wrap and refrigerate the lomi-lomi salmon for at least 30 minutes to allow the flavors to meld together.
6. Once chilled, give the lomi-lomi salmon a final toss and taste test, adjusting the seasoning if necessary.
7. Serve the lomi-lomi salmon chilled as a refreshing appetizer or side dish. Enjoy!

This dish is perfect for hot summer days or anytime you're craving a taste of Hawaii. It's light, flavorful, and incredibly easy to make!

Kalua pork

Ingredients:

- 3-4 pound pork shoulder or pork butt
- 1 tablespoon liquid smoke
- 1 tablespoon sea salt or Hawaiian salt
- 1 tablespoon garlic powder
- 1 tablespoon onion powder
- 1 tablespoon smoked paprika
- 1/2 teaspoon ground black pepper
- Banana leaves or ti leaves (optional, for wrapping)
- Steamed white rice, for serving
- Sliced green onions, for garnish (optional)

Instructions:

1. Preheat your oven to 325°F (160°C) or set your slow cooker to low heat.
2. Rinse the pork shoulder under cold water and pat it dry with paper towels. If desired, score the fat cap of the pork shoulder with a sharp knife to help the seasonings penetrate.
3. In a small bowl, mix together the liquid smoke, sea salt, garlic powder, onion powder, smoked paprika, and black pepper to make a seasoning rub.
4. Rub the seasoning mixture all over the pork shoulder, making sure to coat it evenly.
5. If you have banana leaves or ti leaves, you can use them to wrap the pork shoulder before cooking. Otherwise, you can simply place the pork shoulder in a roasting pan or slow cooker.
6. If using an oven, cover the roasting pan tightly with aluminum foil. If using a slow cooker, cover it with the lid.
7. Cook the pork shoulder in the preheated oven for 6-8 hours, or until it is fork-tender and falls apart easily. If using a slow cooker, cook on low heat for 8-10 hours.
8. Once the pork shoulder is cooked, remove it from the oven or slow cooker and transfer it to a cutting board. Use two forks to shred the pork into bite-sized pieces.

9. Serve the Kalua pork hot, accompanied by steamed white rice. Garnish with sliced green onions, if desired.
10. Enjoy your homemade Kalua pork, a delicious taste of Hawaii right in your own home!

This dish is perfect for luaus, potlucks, or anytime you're craving a taste of the islands.

It's flavorful, tender, and incredibly satisfying!

Poi

Ingredients:

- 2-3 large taro roots
- Water

Instructions:

1. Start by peeling the taro roots to remove the tough outer skin.
2. Cut the taro roots into small cubes and rinse them under cold water to remove any dirt or debris.
3. Place the taro cubes in a large pot and cover them with water. Make sure the water level is about 2 inches above the taro cubes.
4. Bring the water to a boil over high heat, then reduce the heat to medium-low and simmer the taro cubes for 30-45 minutes, or until they are very tender and easily pierced with a fork.
5. Once the taro cubes are cooked, drain them and transfer them to a large bowl or food processor.
6. Use a potato masher or food processor to mash the cooked taro cubes into a smooth, creamy consistency. Add small amounts of water as needed to achieve the desired texture.
7. Continue mashing or blending the taro until it reaches the consistency of a thick paste. This is your poi.
8. Serve the poi immediately as a side dish or accompaniment to other Hawaiian dishes.

Poi can be served at different stages of fermentation, ranging from fresh (sweet) to slightly fermented (sour). The longer it sits, the more it ferments and becomes sour. Some people prefer it fresh, while others enjoy the tanginess of slightly fermented poi.

Enjoy your homemade poi as a traditional Hawaiian treat!

Shoyu

Ingredients:

- 1 cup soy sauce
- 1/4 cup mirin (Japanese sweet rice wine)
- 1/4 cup sake (Japanese rice wine)
- 1 tablespoon sugar
- 1 teaspoon grated fresh ginger (optional)

Instructions:

1. In a small saucepan, combine the soy sauce, mirin, sake, sugar, and grated ginger (if using).
2. Heat the mixture over medium heat, stirring occasionally, until the sugar has dissolved and the sauce is heated through.
3. Once the sauce is heated through, remove it from the heat and let it cool to room temperature.
4. Transfer the shoyu sauce to a clean glass bottle or jar for storage.
5. Store the shoyu sauce in the refrigerator for up to several weeks. The flavors will continue to develop over time.

Homemade shoyu sauce is incredibly versatile and can be used to enhance the flavor of a wide variety of dishes, including stir-fries, marinades, dipping sauces, and more. Adjust the ingredients to suit your taste preferences, adding more or less sugar or ginger as desired. Enjoy your homemade shoyu sauce!

Guava

Ingredients:

For the crust:

- 1 1/2 cups all-purpose flour
- 1/2 cup granulated sugar
- 1/2 teaspoon baking powder
- 1/4 teaspoon salt
- 1/2 cup unsalted butter, chilled and cut into small pieces
- 1 egg, lightly beaten
- 1 teaspoon vanilla extract

For the guava filling:

- 2 cups guava paste, chopped into small pieces
- 1/4 cup water
- 1 tablespoon lime juice
- Zest of 1 lime

Instructions:

1. Preheat your oven to 350°F (175°C). Grease and line a 9x9 inch baking pan with parchment paper, leaving some overhang on the sides for easy removal later.
2. In a large mixing bowl, whisk together the flour, sugar, baking powder, and salt until well combined.
3. Add the chilled butter pieces to the flour mixture. Using a pastry cutter or your fingers, work the butter into the flour until the mixture resembles coarse crumbs.
4. Add the beaten egg and vanilla extract to the flour mixture. Stir until the dough comes together and forms a ball.
5. Press the dough evenly into the bottom of the prepared baking pan. Use your hands or the back of a spoon to smooth it out.
6. In a small saucepan, combine the chopped guava paste, water, lime juice, and lime zest. Cook over medium heat, stirring constantly, until the guava paste has melted and the mixture is smooth. Remove from heat and let it cool slightly.

7. Pour the guava filling over the crust in the baking pan, spreading it out evenly.
8. Bake in the preheated oven for 25-30 minutes, or until the edges are lightly golden brown and the filling is set.
9. Remove from the oven and let the guava bars cool completely in the pan on a wire rack.
10. Once cooled, use the parchment paper overhang to lift the guava bars out of the pan. Place them on a cutting board and slice into squares or bars.
11. Serve the guava bars at room temperature and enjoy!

These guava bars are sweet, tangy, and utterly delicious. They make a perfect snack or dessert for any occasion. Enjoy!

Lilikoi (passion fruit)

Ingredients:

For the crust:

- 1 1/2 cups graham cracker crumbs
- 1/4 cup granulated sugar
- 1/2 cup unsalted butter, melted

For the filling:

- 16 oz (2 packages) cream cheese, softened
- 2/3 cup granulated sugar
- 2 large eggs
- 1/3 cup lilikoi (passion fruit) puree (strained)
- 1 teaspoon vanilla extract

For the topping:

- 1/2 cup lilikoi (passion fruit) puree (strained)
- 1/4 cup granulated sugar
- 1 tablespoon cornstarch
- 1/4 cup water

Instructions:

1. Preheat your oven to 325°F (160°C). Line an 8x8 inch baking pan with parchment paper, leaving some overhang on the sides for easy removal later.
2. In a mixing bowl, combine the graham cracker crumbs, sugar, and melted butter. Stir until the crumbs are evenly coated with butter.
3. Press the crumb mixture evenly into the bottom of the prepared baking pan. Use the back of a spoon or the bottom of a glass to press it down firmly.

4. In another mixing bowl, beat the softened cream cheese and sugar together until smooth and creamy.
5. Add the eggs, one at a time, beating well after each addition. Mix in the lilikoi puree and vanilla extract until smooth.
6. Pour the cream cheese mixture over the graham cracker crust in the baking pan. Spread it out evenly with a spatula.
7. Bake in the preheated oven for 25-30 minutes, or until the edges are set but the center is slightly jiggly.
8. While the cheesecake bars are baking, make the lilikoi topping. In a small saucepan, combine the lilikoi puree, sugar, cornstarch, and water. Cook over medium heat, stirring constantly, until the mixture thickens and comes to a gentle boil. Remove from heat and let it cool slightly.
9. Once the cheesecake bars are done baking, remove them from the oven and let them cool in the pan on a wire rack for about 10 minutes.
10. Carefully spread the lilikoi topping over the partially cooled cheesecake layer.
11. Allow the cheesecake bars to cool completely in the pan, then refrigerate for at least 2-3 hours or until chilled and firm.
12. Once chilled, use the parchment paper overhang to lift the cheesecake bars out of the pan. Cut into squares or bars using a sharp knife.
13. Serve the lilikoi cheesecake bars chilled and enjoy the tropical flavors!

These lilikoi cheesecake bars are creamy, tangy, and bursting with the exotic flavor of passion fruit. They're perfect for any occasion and are sure to impress your friends and family!

Huli-huli chicken

Ingredients:

- 4 boneless, skinless chicken breasts
- 1 cup pineapple juice
- 1/2 cup soy sauce
- 1/4 cup ketchup
- 1/4 cup brown sugar
- 2 tablespoons rice vinegar
- 2 cloves garlic, minced
- 1 teaspoon grated fresh ginger
- 1/2 teaspoon sesame oil
- Salt and pepper, to taste
- Pineapple slices (optional, for garnish)
- Green onions, chopped (optional, for garnish)

Instructions:

1. In a mixing bowl, whisk together pineapple juice, soy sauce, ketchup, brown sugar, rice vinegar, minced garlic, grated ginger, sesame oil, salt, and pepper. This will be your marinade.
2. Place the chicken breasts in a shallow dish or a large resealable plastic bag. Pour the marinade over the chicken, making sure it's evenly coated. Marinate in the refrigerator for at least 2 hours, or preferably overnight, turning occasionally to ensure even marination.
3. Preheat your grill to medium-high heat. Lightly oil the grill grates to prevent sticking.
4. Remove the chicken from the marinade and discard any excess marinade. Grill the chicken breasts for about 6-8 minutes on each side, or until they are cooked through and have nice grill marks. Baste the chicken with the remaining marinade during grilling for extra flavor.
5. Once the chicken is cooked through, remove it from the grill and let it rest for a few minutes before serving.
6. Optionally, garnish the grilled chicken with pineapple slices and chopped green onions for a traditional Hawaiian touch.

7. Serve the huli-huli chicken hot with your favorite side dishes, such as rice, grilled vegetables, or a tropical salad.

Enjoy your homemade huli-huli chicken with family and friends at your next barbecue or Hawaiian-themed gathering!

Haupia (coconut pudding)

Ingredients:

- 2 cups coconut milk
- 1/2 cup sugar
- 1/2 cup water
- 1/2 cup cornstarch
- Toasted coconut flakes, for garnish (optional)

Instructions:

1. In a saucepan, combine the coconut milk and sugar over medium heat. Stir until the sugar is dissolved and the mixture is heated through.
2. In a small bowl, dissolve the cornstarch in water to create a slurry.
3. Slowly pour the cornstarch slurry into the coconut milk mixture, whisking continuously to prevent lumps from forming.
4. Bring the mixture to a gentle boil, then reduce the heat to low. Cook, stirring constantly, for about 5-7 minutes, or until the mixture thickens to a pudding-like consistency.
5. Once thickened, remove the saucepan from the heat and pour the haupia mixture into a greased 8x8-inch square baking dish or individual serving cups.
6. Let the haupia cool at room temperature for about 30 minutes, then transfer it to the refrigerator to chill and set for at least 2 hours, or until firm.
7. Once chilled and set, cut the haupia into squares or scoop it into serving bowls. Garnish with toasted coconut flakes, if desired.
8. Serve the haupia cold as a refreshing and delicious dessert.

Enjoy the creamy coconut goodness of homemade haupia as a delightful treat on its own or alongside other Hawaiian desserts!

Lau Lau

Ingredients:

- 8 large taro leaves
- 1 lb pork butt or pork shoulder, cut into chunks
- 1/2 lb salted butterfish or cod, cut into chunks
- Sea salt, to taste
- Ti leaves or banana leaves (optional, for wrapping)
- Butcher's twine or toothpicks (for securing the wraps)

Instructions:

1. Rinse the taro leaves under cold water to remove any dirt or debris. Trim the stems and tough ribs from the leaves, then set them aside.
2. Season the pork and fish with sea salt to taste.
3. Take two taro leaves and place them in a cross shape, one on top of the other, with the stems facing opposite directions.
4. Place a few pieces of pork and fish in the center of the taro leaves.
5. Fold the sides of the taro leaves over the pork and fish, then fold the top and bottom of the leaves over to form a bundle.
6. If using ti leaves or banana leaves, wrap the bundles with the leaves to secure them. Use butcher's twine or toothpicks to tie the bundles closed.
7. Place the wrapped lau lau bundles in a steamer basket or on a rack in a large pot. Add water to the pot, making sure it doesn't touch the bottom of the steamer basket.
8. Cover the pot with a lid and steam the lau lau bundles for about 3-4 hours, or until the pork is tender and cooked through.
9. Once cooked, carefully remove the lau lau bundles from the steamer. Allow them to cool slightly before unwrapping and serving.
10. Serve the lau lau hot, either as a main dish or as part of a traditional Hawaiian feast (luau).

Enjoy the delicious flavors of homemade pork lau lau, a beloved dish in Hawaiian cuisine!

Mahi mahi

Ingredients:

- 4 mahi-mahi fillets (6-8 ounces each)
- 2 tablespoons olive oil
- 2 cloves garlic, minced
- 1 teaspoon lemon zest
- 1 tablespoon lemon juice
- 1 teaspoon paprika
- 1/2 teaspoon cumin
- Salt and pepper, to taste
- Lemon wedges, for serving
- Fresh chopped parsley, for garnish

Instructions:

1. Preheat your grill to medium-high heat.
2. In a small bowl, whisk together the olive oil, minced garlic, lemon zest, lemon juice, paprika, cumin, salt, and pepper to create a marinade.
3. Pat the mahi-mahi fillets dry with paper towels. Place them in a shallow dish or a large resealable plastic bag.
4. Pour the marinade over the mahi-mahi fillets, making sure they are evenly coated. Allow the fish to marinate for about 20-30 minutes in the refrigerator.
5. Remove the mahi-mahi fillets from the marinade and discard any excess marinade.
6. Lightly oil the grill grates to prevent sticking. Place the mahi-mahi fillets on the preheated grill.
7. Grill the mahi-mahi fillets for about 4-5 minutes on each side, or until they are opaque and easily flake with a fork. Be careful not to overcook the fish to maintain its moistness and flavor.
8. Once cooked through, remove the mahi-mahi fillets from the grill and transfer them to a serving platter.
9. Garnish the grilled mahi-mahi with fresh chopped parsley and serve hot with lemon wedges on the side.
10. Enjoy your grilled mahi-mahi with your favorite side dishes, such as steamed rice, grilled vegetables, or a fresh salad.

Grilled mahi-mahi is a healthy and flavorful dish that's perfect for a summer barbecue or a weeknight dinner. Enjoy!

Ahi tuna

Ingredients:

- 2 ahi tuna steaks (6-8 ounces each)
- 2 tablespoons soy sauce
- 1 tablespoon sesame oil
- 1 tablespoon honey or brown sugar
- 1 tablespoon rice vinegar
- 1 teaspoon grated fresh ginger
- 1 clove garlic, minced
- 1 tablespoon sesame seeds
- Salt and pepper, to taste
- 2 tablespoons vegetable oil (for searing)
- Sliced green onions, for garnish (optional)
- Sliced avocado, for serving (optional)
- Cooked white or brown rice, for serving

Instructions:

1. In a small bowl, whisk together the soy sauce, sesame oil, honey or brown sugar, rice vinegar, grated ginger, minced garlic, sesame seeds, salt, and pepper to create a marinade.
2. Place the ahi tuna steaks in a shallow dish or a large resealable plastic bag. Pour the marinade over the tuna steaks, making sure they are evenly coated. Allow the tuna to marinate for about 15-30 minutes in the refrigerator.
3. Remove the ahi tuna steaks from the marinade and discard any excess marinade.
4. Heat the vegetable oil in a large skillet or cast-iron pan over high heat until it begins to smoke slightly.
5. Carefully place the ahi tuna steaks in the hot skillet or pan. Sear the tuna for about 1-2 minutes on each side, depending on the thickness of the steaks, for medium-rare doneness. Adjust the cooking time to your desired level of doneness.
6. Once seared, remove the ahi tuna steaks from the skillet or pan and transfer them to a cutting board. Allow the tuna to rest for a few minutes before slicing.
7. Slice the seared ahi tuna steaks thinly against the grain.

8. Serve the seared ahi tuna slices over cooked rice, garnished with sliced green onions and sliced avocado if desired.
9. Enjoy your delicious seared ahi tuna with soy-ginger marinade as a flavorful and healthy meal!

Seared ahi tuna is best served immediately while it's still warm and tender. It pairs well with a variety of side dishes, such as steamed vegetables, Asian slaw, or a fresh salad.

Ono (wahoo fish)

Ingredients:

- 4 ono fillets (6-8 ounces each)
- 2 tablespoons olive oil
- 2 cloves garlic, minced
- 1 tablespoon lemon juice
- 1 teaspoon lemon zest
- 1 teaspoon paprika
- 1/2 teaspoon dried thyme
- Salt and pepper, to taste
- Lemon wedges, for serving
- Fresh chopped parsley, for garnish

Instructions:

1. Preheat your grill to medium-high heat.
2. In a small bowl, whisk together the olive oil, minced garlic, lemon juice, lemon zest, paprika, dried thyme, salt, and pepper to create a marinade.
3. Pat the ono fillets dry with paper towels. Place them in a shallow dish or a large resealable plastic bag.
4. Pour the marinade over the ono fillets, making sure they are evenly coated. Allow the fish to marinate for about 20-30 minutes in the refrigerator.
5. Remove the ono fillets from the marinade and discard any excess marinade.
6. Lightly oil the grill grates to prevent sticking. Place the ono fillets on the preheated grill.
7. Grill the ono fillets for about 4-5 minutes on each side, or until they are opaque and easily flake with a fork. Be careful not to overcook the fish to maintain its moistness and flavor.
8. Once cooked through, remove the ono fillets from the grill and transfer them to a serving platter.
9. Garnish the grilled ono with fresh chopped parsley and serve hot with lemon wedges on the side.
10. Enjoy your grilled ono as a flavorful and healthy main dish!

Grilled ono is a delicious and versatile fish that pairs well with a variety of side dishes, such as steamed vegetables, rice pilaf, or a fresh salad. It's perfect for a summer barbecue or a weeknight dinner.

Huli-huli sauce

Ingredients:

- 1 cup soy sauce
- 1/2 cup brown sugar
- 1/4 cup ketchup
- 1/4 cup pineapple juice
- 1/4 cup rice vinegar
- 2 cloves garlic, minced
- 1 tablespoon grated fresh ginger
- 1 tablespoon sesame oil
- 1 teaspoon Worcestershire sauce
- 1/2 teaspoon smoked paprika (optional, for a smoky flavor)
- Salt and pepper, to taste

Instructions:

1. In a medium saucepan, combine the soy sauce, brown sugar, ketchup, pineapple juice, rice vinegar, minced garlic, grated ginger, sesame oil, Worcestershire sauce, and smoked paprika (if using).
2. Place the saucepan over medium heat and bring the mixture to a simmer, stirring occasionally.
3. Reduce the heat to low and let the sauce simmer gently for about 10-15 minutes, or until it has thickened slightly and the flavors have melded together.
4. Taste the sauce and adjust the seasoning with salt and pepper, if needed.
5. Once the huli-huli sauce has reached your desired consistency and flavor, remove the saucepan from the heat and let the sauce cool completely.
6. Once cooled, transfer the huli-huli sauce to a jar or airtight container. You can store it in the refrigerator for up to 1 week.
7. To use the huli-huli sauce as a marinade, simply place your choice of meat (such as chicken, pork, or beef) in a shallow dish or resealable plastic bag. Pour the marinade over the meat, making sure it is evenly coated. Cover the dish or seal the bag and refrigerate for at least 2 hours, or overnight, to allow the flavors to penetrate the meat.

8. When ready to cook, remove the meat from the marinade and discard any excess marinade. Grill the meat as desired, basting with additional huli-huli sauce while cooking for extra flavor and moisture.
9. Serve the grilled meat hot, garnished with chopped green onions or sesame seeds, if desired.

Enjoy the delicious flavor of homemade huli-huli sauce on your grilled meats for a taste of Hawaiian barbecue!

Teriyaki

Ingredients:

- 1/2 cup soy sauce
- 1/4 cup water
- 2 tablespoons brown sugar
- 2 tablespoons honey
- 1 tablespoon rice vinegar
- 1 clove garlic, minced
- 1 teaspoon grated fresh ginger
- 1 tablespoon cornstarch (optional, for thickening)

Instructions:

1. In a small saucepan, combine the soy sauce, water, brown sugar, honey, rice vinegar, minced garlic, and grated ginger.
2. Place the saucepan over medium heat and bring the mixture to a simmer, stirring occasionally to dissolve the sugar.
3. If you prefer a thicker sauce, you can mix the cornstarch with 1-2 tablespoons of water to create a slurry. Stir the cornstarch slurry into the simmering sauce and continue to cook for another 1-2 minutes, or until the sauce has thickened to your desired consistency.
4. Once the teriyaki sauce has thickened (if using cornstarch), remove the saucepan from the heat and let the sauce cool slightly.
5. Taste the teriyaki sauce and adjust the seasoning if needed. You can add more sugar for sweetness or more soy sauce for saltiness, depending on your preference.
6. Once cooled, transfer the teriyaki sauce to a jar or airtight container. You can store it in the refrigerator for up to 1 week.

To use the teriyaki sauce:

- Use it as a marinade for chicken, beef, pork, tofu, or seafood. Place your choice of protein in a shallow dish or resealable plastic bag, pour the teriyaki sauce over it, and let it marinate in the refrigerator for at least 30 minutes, or up to overnight.

- Use it as a glaze for grilled meats, seafood, or vegetables. Brush the teriyaki sauce onto the food during the last few minutes of grilling, allowing it to caramelize and create a deliciously sticky glaze.
- Use it as a stir-fry sauce for vegetables, tofu, or noodles. Heat a tablespoon of oil in a skillet or wok, add your choice of ingredients, and stir-fry until cooked through. Then, add the teriyaki sauce and toss to coat everything evenly.

Enjoy the homemade teriyaki sauce on your favorite dishes for a deliciously flavorful meal!

Teriyaki-glazed

Ingredients:

- 4 salmon fillets (6-8 ounces each)
- Salt and pepper, to taste
- 1 tablespoon vegetable oil
- Sesame seeds, for garnish (optional)
- Sliced green onions, for garnish (optional)

For the teriyaki glaze:

- 1/2 cup soy sauce
- 1/4 cup water
- 2 tablespoons brown sugar
- 2 tablespoons honey
- 1 tablespoon rice vinegar
- 1 clove garlic, minced
- 1 teaspoon grated fresh ginger
- 1 tablespoon cornstarch (optional, for thickening)
- Sesame seeds, for garnish (optional)
- Sliced green onions, for garnish (optional)

Instructions:

1. Preheat your oven to 400°F (200°C).
2. Season the salmon fillets with salt and pepper on both sides.
3. In a small saucepan, combine the soy sauce, water, brown sugar, honey, rice vinegar, minced garlic, and grated ginger to make the teriyaki glaze.
4. Place the saucepan over medium heat and bring the mixture to a simmer, stirring occasionally.
5. If you prefer a thicker glaze, you can mix the cornstarch with 1-2 tablespoons of water to create a slurry. Stir the cornstarch slurry into the simmering sauce and continue to cook for another 1-2 minutes, or until the sauce has thickened to your desired consistency.

6. Heat the vegetable oil in an oven-safe skillet over medium-high heat. Once hot, add the salmon fillets to the skillet, skin-side down, and sear for about 2-3 minutes, or until golden brown.
7. Flip the salmon fillets over and brush them generously with the teriyaki glaze.
8. Transfer the skillet to the preheated oven and bake for 8-10 minutes, or until the salmon is cooked through and flakes easily with a fork.
9. Once cooked, remove the skillet from the oven and brush the salmon fillets with more teriyaki glaze.
10. Garnish the teriyaki-glazed salmon with sesame seeds and sliced green onions, if desired, before serving.
11. Serve the teriyaki-glazed salmon hot with your favorite side dishes, such as steamed rice and vegetables.

Enjoy the delicious and flavorful teriyaki-glazed salmon for a satisfying meal!

Teriyaki chicken

Ingredients:

- 4 boneless, skinless chicken breasts
- Salt and pepper, to taste
- 1 tablespoon vegetable oil
- Sesame seeds, for garnish (optional)
- Sliced green onions, for garnish (optional)

For the teriyaki sauce:

- 1/2 cup soy sauce
- 1/4 cup water
- 2 tablespoons brown sugar
- 2 tablespoons honey
- 1 tablespoon rice vinegar
- 1 clove garlic, minced
- 1 teaspoon grated fresh ginger
- 1 tablespoon cornstarch (optional, for thickening)

Instructions:

1. Season the chicken breasts with salt and pepper on both sides.
2. In a small saucepan, combine the soy sauce, water, brown sugar, honey, rice vinegar, minced garlic, and grated ginger to make the teriyaki sauce.
3. Place the saucepan over medium heat and bring the mixture to a simmer, stirring occasionally.
4. If you prefer a thicker sauce, you can mix the cornstarch with 1-2 tablespoons of water to create a slurry. Stir the cornstarch slurry into the simmering sauce and continue to cook for another 1-2 minutes, or until the sauce has thickened to your desired consistency.
5. Heat the vegetable oil in a large skillet over medium-high heat. Once hot, add the chicken breasts to the skillet and cook for 4-5 minutes on each side, or until golden brown and cooked through.

6. Brush the cooked chicken breasts generously with the teriyaki sauce, reserving some sauce for serving.
7. Continue to cook the chicken breasts for another 1-2 minutes, allowing the sauce to caramelize and coat the chicken.
8. Once cooked, remove the chicken breasts from the skillet and let them rest for a few minutes.
9. Slice the teriyaki chicken breasts and garnish with sesame seeds and sliced green onions, if desired.
10. Serve the teriyaki chicken hot with steamed rice and vegetables, drizzling extra teriyaki sauce over the top.

Enjoy the delicious and flavorful teriyaki chicken for a satisfying meal!

Teriyaki beef

Ingredients:

- 1 lb (450g) beef steak (sirloin, flank, or ribeye), thinly sliced against the grain
- Salt and pepper, to taste
- 2 tablespoons vegetable oil
- Sesame seeds, for garnish (optional)
- Sliced green onions, for garnish (optional)

For the teriyaki sauce:

- 1/2 cup soy sauce
- 1/4 cup water
- 2 tablespoons brown sugar
- 2 tablespoons honey
- 1 tablespoon rice vinegar
- 1 clove garlic, minced
- 1 teaspoon grated fresh ginger
- 1 tablespoon cornstarch (optional, for thickening)

Instructions:

1. In a small saucepan, combine the soy sauce, water, brown sugar, honey, rice vinegar, minced garlic, and grated ginger to make the teriyaki sauce.
2. Place the saucepan over medium heat and bring the mixture to a simmer, stirring occasionally.
3. If you prefer a thicker sauce, you can mix the cornstarch with 1-2 tablespoons of water to create a slurry. Stir the cornstarch slurry into the simmering sauce and continue to cook for another 1-2 minutes, or until the sauce has thickened to your desired consistency.
4. Season the thinly sliced beef with salt and pepper on both sides.
5. Heat the vegetable oil in a large skillet or wok over high heat. Once hot, add the sliced beef to the skillet in a single layer, making sure not to overcrowd the pan.
6. Cook the beef for 1-2 minutes on each side, or until browned and caramelized.
7. Pour the teriyaki sauce over the beef in the skillet and toss to coat evenly.

8. Continue to cook the beef for another 1-2 minutes, allowing the sauce to thicken and coat the beef.
9. Once cooked through and the sauce has thickened, remove the skillet from the heat.
10. Garnish the teriyaki beef with sesame seeds and sliced green onions, if desired.
11. Serve the teriyaki beef hot with steamed rice and vegetables.

Enjoy the delicious and flavorful teriyaki beef for a satisfying meal!

Teriyaki salmon

Ingredients:

- 4 salmon fillets (6-8 ounces each), skin-on or skinless
- Salt and pepper, to taste
- 2 tablespoons vegetable oil
- Sesame seeds, for garnish (optional)
- Sliced green onions, for garnish (optional)

For the teriyaki sauce:

- 1/2 cup soy sauce
- 1/4 cup water
- 2 tablespoons brown sugar
- 2 tablespoons honey
- 1 tablespoon rice vinegar
- 1 clove garlic, minced
- 1 teaspoon grated fresh ginger
- 1 tablespoon cornstarch (optional, for thickening)

Instructions:

1. Preheat your oven to 400°F (200°C).
2. Season the salmon fillets with salt and pepper on both sides.
3. In a small saucepan, combine the soy sauce, water, brown sugar, honey, rice vinegar, minced garlic, and grated ginger to make the teriyaki sauce.
4. Place the saucepan over medium heat and bring the mixture to a simmer, stirring occasionally.
5. If you prefer a thicker sauce, you can mix the cornstarch with 1-2 tablespoons of water to create a slurry. Stir the cornstarch slurry into the simmering sauce and continue to cook for another 1-2 minutes, or until the sauce has thickened to your desired consistency.
6. Heat the vegetable oil in an oven-safe skillet over medium-high heat. Once hot, add the salmon fillets to the skillet, skin-side down if using skin-on fillets.
7. Sear the salmon fillets for about 2-3 minutes, or until golden brown on the bottom.
8. Flip the salmon fillets over and brush them generously with the teriyaki sauce.

9. Transfer the skillet to the preheated oven and bake for 8-10 minutes, or until the salmon is cooked through and flakes easily with a fork.
10. Once cooked, remove the skillet from the oven and brush the salmon fillets with more teriyaki sauce.
11. Garnish the teriyaki salmon with sesame seeds and sliced green onions, if desired, before serving.
12. Serve the teriyaki salmon hot with your favorite side dishes, such as steamed rice and vegetables.

Enjoy the delicious and flavorful teriyaki salmon for a satisfying meal!

Huli-huli pineapple

Ingredients:

- 1 ripe pineapple, peeled, cored, and cut into wedges
- 1/2 cup soy sauce
- 1/4 cup pineapple juice
- 1/4 cup brown sugar
- 2 tablespoons honey
- 2 tablespoons rice vinegar
- 1 clove garlic, minced
- 1 teaspoon grated fresh ginger
- 1 tablespoon cornstarch (optional, for thickening)
- Vegetable oil, for grilling

Instructions:

1. In a small saucepan, combine the soy sauce, pineapple juice, brown sugar, honey, rice vinegar, minced garlic, and grated ginger to make the huli-huli marinade.
2. Place the saucepan over medium heat and bring the mixture to a simmer, stirring occasionally.
3. If you prefer a thicker marinade, you can mix the cornstarch with 1-2 tablespoons of water to create a slurry. Stir the cornstarch slurry into the simmering marinade and continue to cook for another 1-2 minutes, or until the marinade has thickened to your desired consistency.
4. Remove the marinade from the heat and let it cool to room temperature.
5. Place the pineapple wedges in a shallow dish or resealable plastic bag, and pour the cooled huli-huli marinade over the pineapple. Make sure the pineapple is well coated in the marinade.
6. Cover the dish or seal the bag, and refrigerate the pineapple for at least 1 hour, or preferably overnight, to marinate.
7. Preheat your grill to medium-high heat.
8. Remove the pineapple wedges from the marinade and shake off any excess marinade.
9. Lightly brush the grill grates with vegetable oil to prevent sticking.
10. Grill the pineapple wedges for 3-4 minutes on each side, or until grill marks form and the pineapple is caramelized and slightly softened.

11. Once grilled, remove the pineapple wedges from the grill and serve immediately.
12. Garnish the huli-huli pineapple with fresh mint leaves or toasted coconut flakes, if desired, for added flavor and presentation.

Enjoy the delicious huli-huli pineapple as a side dish, dessert, or snack!

Huli-huli sauce

Ingredients:

- 1 cup soy sauce
- 1/2 cup pineapple juice
- 1/2 cup brown sugar
- 1/4 cup ketchup
- 1/4 cup rice vinegar
- 2 tablespoons honey
- 2 cloves garlic, minced
- 1 tablespoon grated fresh ginger
- 1 teaspoon sesame oil
- 1/2 teaspoon black pepper

Instructions:

1. In a medium saucepan, combine the soy sauce, pineapple juice, brown sugar, ketchup, rice vinegar, honey, minced garlic, grated ginger, sesame oil, and black pepper.
2. Place the saucepan over medium heat and bring the mixture to a simmer, stirring occasionally.
3. Reduce the heat to low and let the sauce simmer gently for about 10-15 minutes, or until it has thickened slightly and the flavors have melded together.
4. Taste the sauce and adjust the seasoning, if necessary, by adding more soy sauce for saltiness, brown sugar for sweetness, or rice vinegar for tanginess.
5. Once the sauce reaches your desired consistency and flavor, remove it from the heat and let it cool to room temperature.
6. Transfer the huli-huli sauce to a glass jar or container with a tight-fitting lid, and store it in the refrigerator until ready to use.
7. Before using the huli-huli sauce as a marinade, give it a good stir or shake to recombine any separated ingredients.
8. Use the huli-huli sauce to marinate chicken, pork, beef, or even tofu before grilling, roasting, or baking for a delicious Hawaiian-inspired flavor.

Enjoy the homemade huli-huli sauce on your favorite grilled dishes!

Grilled pineapple

Ingredients:

- 1 ripe pineapple
- 2 tablespoons brown sugar (optional)
- 1 teaspoon ground cinnamon (optional)
- Vegetable oil, for grilling

Instructions:

1. Preheat your grill to medium-high heat.
2. Slice off the top and bottom of the pineapple, then stand it upright on a cutting board. Use a sharp knife to carefully slice off the outer skin in strips, working your way around the pineapple.
3. Once the skin is removed, lay the pineapple on its side and cut it into slices or wedges, about 1/2 to 1 inch thick.
4. If desired, you can mix the brown sugar and ground cinnamon together in a small bowl.
5. Lightly brush both sides of the pineapple slices with vegetable oil to prevent sticking.
6. If using the brown sugar and cinnamon mixture, sprinkle it evenly over both sides of the pineapple slices.
7. Place the pineapple slices directly on the preheated grill grates.
8. Grill the pineapple slices for 2-3 minutes on each side, or until grill marks form and the pineapple is heated through and caramelized.
9. Once grilled to your liking, remove the pineapple slices from the grill and transfer them to a serving platter.
10. Serve the grilled pineapple slices hot as a side dish, dessert, or topping for grilled meats, burgers, or salads.

Enjoy the delicious flavor of grilled pineapple on its own or as part of your favorite dishes!

Coconut shrimp

Ingredients:

- 1 lb (about 450g) large shrimp, peeled and deveined, tails left on
- 1 cup all-purpose flour
- 1 teaspoon salt
- 1/2 teaspoon black pepper
- 2 large eggs
- 1 cup shredded coconut (sweetened or unsweetened)
- 1 cup panko breadcrumbs (or regular breadcrumbs)
- Vegetable oil, for frying

For the dipping sauce (optional):

- 1/2 cup sweet chili sauce
- 2 tablespoons mayonnaise
- 1 tablespoon lime juice
- 1 teaspoon soy sauce

Instructions:

1. In a shallow dish, whisk together the flour, salt, and black pepper. In another shallow dish, beat the eggs.
2. In a third shallow dish, combine the shredded coconut and panko breadcrumbs.
3. Hold a shrimp by the tail and dredge it in the flour mixture, shaking off any excess. Dip it into the beaten eggs, allowing any excess to drip off, then coat it in the coconut-breadcrumb mixture, pressing gently to adhere. Repeat with the remaining shrimp.
4. In a large skillet or frying pan, heat about 1 inch of vegetable oil over medium-high heat until hot but not smoking.
5. Working in batches, carefully add the coated shrimp to the hot oil, making sure not to overcrowd the pan. Fry the shrimp for 2-3 minutes on each side, or until golden brown and crispy. Use tongs to flip them halfway through cooking.
6. Once cooked, transfer the shrimp to a plate lined with paper towels to drain any excess oil.

7. Repeat the frying process with the remaining shrimp, adding more oil to the pan if needed.
8. While the shrimp are frying, you can prepare the dipping sauce by whisking together the sweet chili sauce, mayonnaise, lime juice, and soy sauce in a small bowl.
9. Serve the crispy coconut shrimp hot, with the dipping sauce on the side.

Enjoy the delicious flavor and crispy texture of homemade coconut shrimp as a tasty appetizer or main dish!

Coconut chicken

Ingredients:

- 4 boneless, skinless chicken breasts, cut into strips or nuggets
- 1 cup all-purpose flour
- 1 teaspoon salt
- 1/2 teaspoon black pepper
- 2 large eggs
- 1 cup shredded coconut (sweetened or unsweetened)
- 1 cup panko breadcrumbs (or regular breadcrumbs)
- Vegetable oil, for frying

For the dipping sauce (optional):

- 1/2 cup sweet chili sauce
- 2 tablespoons mayonnaise
- 1 tablespoon lime juice
- 1 teaspoon soy sauce

Instructions:

1. In a shallow dish, whisk together the flour, salt, and black pepper. In another shallow dish, beat the eggs.
2. In a third shallow dish, combine the shredded coconut and panko breadcrumbs.
3. Dip each chicken strip or nugget into the flour mixture, shaking off any excess. Then, dip it into the beaten eggs, allowing any excess to drip off. Finally, coat it in the coconut-breadcrumb mixture, pressing gently to adhere. Repeat with the remaining chicken pieces.
4. In a large skillet or frying pan, heat about 1 inch of vegetable oil over medium-high heat until hot but not smoking.
5. Working in batches, carefully add the coated chicken pieces to the hot oil, making sure not to overcrowd the pan. Fry the chicken for 3-4 minutes on each side, or until golden brown and cooked through. Use tongs to flip them halfway through cooking.

6. Once cooked, transfer the chicken pieces to a plate lined with paper towels to drain any excess oil.
7. While the chicken is frying, you can prepare the dipping sauce by whisking together the sweet chili sauce, mayonnaise, lime juice, and soy sauce in a small bowl.
8. Serve the crispy coconut chicken hot, with the dipping sauce on the side.

Enjoy the delicious flavor and crispy texture of homemade coconut chicken as a tasty main dish or appetizer!

Loco moco

Ingredients:

For the hamburger patties:

- 1 lb ground beef
- Salt and pepper, to taste
- 1 tablespoon Worcestershire sauce
- 1 tablespoon soy sauce
- 1 teaspoon garlic powder
- 1 teaspoon onion powder

For the gravy:

- 2 tablespoons butter
- 2 tablespoons all-purpose flour
- 2 cups beef broth
- 1 tablespoon soy sauce
- Salt and pepper, to taste

For serving:

- Cooked white rice
- Fried eggs

Instructions:

1. In a large bowl, combine the ground beef, salt, pepper, Worcestershire sauce, soy sauce, garlic powder, and onion powder. Mix until well combined, then shape the mixture into hamburger patties.
2. Heat a skillet over medium-high heat and cook the hamburger patties for 4-5 minutes on each side, or until cooked to your desired level of doneness. Remove the patties from the skillet and set aside.

3. In the same skillet, melt the butter over medium heat. Add the flour and whisk constantly until it forms a paste.
4. Gradually whisk in the beef broth and soy sauce, stirring constantly to prevent lumps from forming. Cook the gravy until it thickens, then season with salt and pepper to taste.
5. To assemble the loco moco, place a serving of cooked white rice on a plate. Top with a hamburger patty and a fried egg. Pour the gravy over the top.
6. Serve the loco moco immediately and enjoy!

Feel free to customize your loco moco by adding toppings like sautéed mushrooms, onions, or crispy bacon. It's a comforting and hearty dish that's perfect for any meal of the day!

Musubi

Ingredients:

- 1 can Spam
- 2 cups sushi rice
- 4 sheets nori (seaweed)
- 1/4 cup soy sauce
- 1/4 cup mirin (Japanese sweet rice wine)
- 2 tablespoons sugar
- Furikake seasoning (optional)
- Cooking spray or oil

Instructions:

1. Cook the sushi rice according to the package instructions and let it cool to room temperature.
2. While the rice is cooking, prepare the Spam. Cut the Spam into 8 slices.
3. In a small bowl, mix together the soy sauce, mirin, and sugar to make the marinade.
4. Place the Spam slices in a shallow dish and pour the marinade over them. Let them marinate for about 10-15 minutes.
5. Heat a skillet over medium heat and lightly grease it with cooking spray or oil. Add the Spam slices and cook for 2-3 minutes on each side, or until browned and slightly crispy. Remove from the skillet and set aside.
6. Place a sheet of nori on a clean work surface, shiny side down. Place a musubi mold or a piece of plastic wrap on top of the nori.
7. Fill the mold halfway with sushi rice and press it down firmly to compact it.
8. Place a slice of cooked Spam on top of the rice in the mold.
9. Add another layer of sushi rice on top of the Spam and press it down firmly again.
10. Remove the mold carefully and fold the nori over the musubi, wrapping it tightly.
11. Repeat the process with the remaining Spam slices and rice.
12. If desired, sprinkle furikake seasoning over the top of the musubi for extra flavor.
13. Serve the musubi immediately or wrap each one individually in plastic wrap for later enjoyment.

Musubi is a portable and delicious snack that's perfect for picnics, lunches, or any time you're craving a taste of Hawaii!

Hawaiian roll

Ingredients:

- 4 cups all-purpose flour
- 1/2 cup granulated sugar
- 1 teaspoon salt
- 1 package (2 1/4 teaspoons) active dry yeast
- 1/2 cup unsalted butter, melted
- 3/4 cup pineapple juice
- 2 large eggs

Instructions:

1. In a large mixing bowl, combine 2 cups of flour, sugar, salt, and yeast.
2. In a separate bowl, whisk together the melted butter, pineapple juice, and eggs.
3. Pour the wet ingredients into the dry ingredients and mix until a soft dough forms.
4. Gradually add the remaining flour, 1/4 cup at a time, until the dough pulls away from the sides of the bowl.
5. Turn the dough out onto a lightly floured surface and knead for about 5-7 minutes, or until smooth and elastic.
6. Place the dough in a greased bowl, cover with a clean kitchen towel, and let it rise in a warm, draft-free place for 1-2 hours, or until doubled in size.
7. Punch down the risen dough and divide it into 15-18 equal-sized pieces.
8. Shape each piece of dough into a ball and place them in a greased 9x13-inch baking dish, spacing them evenly apart.
9. Cover the baking dish with plastic wrap and let the rolls rise for another 30-45 minutes, or until doubled in size.
10. Preheat your oven to 350°F (175°C).
11. Bake the rolls in the preheated oven for 20-25 minutes, or until golden brown on top and cooked through.
12. Remove the rolls from the oven and let them cool slightly before serving.

Enjoy your homemade Hawaiian rolls warm with butter or as a delicious addition to any meal!

Hawaiian barbecue

Ingredients:

- 4 boneless, skinless chicken breasts
- 1 cup pineapple juice
- 1/2 cup soy sauce
- 1/4 cup ketchup
- 1/4 cup brown sugar
- 2 cloves garlic, minced
- 1 teaspoon ground ginger
- 1/4 teaspoon black pepper
- Pineapple slices (optional, for garnish)
- Chopped green onions (optional, for garnish)
- Sesame seeds (optional, for garnish)

Instructions:

1. In a mixing bowl, combine the pineapple juice, soy sauce, ketchup, brown sugar, minced garlic, ground ginger, and black pepper. Stir until the sugar is dissolved and the marinade is well mixed.
2. Place the chicken breasts in a resealable plastic bag or a shallow dish. Pour the marinade over the chicken, making sure it's fully submerged. Seal the bag or cover the dish and refrigerate for at least 2 hours, or overnight for best results.
3. Preheat your grill to medium-high heat. Remove the chicken from the marinade and discard any excess marinade.
4. Grill the chicken breasts for 6-8 minutes per side, or until they are cooked through and have nice grill marks. The internal temperature should reach 165°F (75°C).
5. While the chicken is grilling, you can brush it with additional marinade for extra flavor if desired.
6. Once the chicken is cooked, remove it from the grill and let it rest for a few minutes before slicing.
7. Serve the Hawaiian barbecue chicken hot, garnished with pineapple slices, chopped green onions, and sesame seeds if desired.

This Hawaiian barbecue chicken pairs well with rice, grilled vegetables, or a fresh salad. Enjoy the tropical flavors of this delicious dish!

Kona coffee

Ingredients:

- Freshly roasted Kona coffee beans
- Water

Instructions:

1. Grind the Kona coffee beans to a medium-coarse consistency, similar to sea salt.
2. Heat water to just below boiling, around 200°F (93°C).
3. Place the ground coffee into a coffee maker or a pour-over filter.
4. Pour hot water over the coffee grounds, making sure to saturate them evenly. Use a ratio of about 1 to 2 tablespoons of coffee per 6 ounces of water, depending on your preferred strength.
5. Allow the coffee to steep for about 3-4 minutes for optimal flavor extraction.
6. After steeping, gently stir the coffee to mix the grounds.
7. If using a pour-over method, carefully remove the filter containing the grounds.
8. Pour the brewed Kona coffee into a mug and enjoy it as is, or add your preferred sweeteners or creamers to taste.
9. Sit back, relax, and savor the unique taste of Kona coffee!

By following these steps, you can enjoy a delicious cup of Kona coffee brewed to perfection.

Kona blend

Ingredients:

- Freshly roasted Kona coffee beans
- Water

Instructions:

1. Grind the Kona coffee beans to a medium-coarse consistency, similar to sea salt.
2. Heat water to just below boiling, around 200°F (93°C).
3. Place the ground coffee into a coffee maker or a pour-over filter.
4. Pour hot water over the coffee grounds, making sure to saturate them evenly. Use a ratio of about 1 to 2 tablespoons of coffee per 6 ounces of water, depending on your preferred strength.
5. Allow the coffee to steep for about 3-4 minutes for optimal flavor extraction.
6. After steeping, gently stir the coffee to mix the grounds.
7. If using a pour-over method, carefully remove the filter containing the grounds.
8. Pour the brewed Kona coffee into a mug and enjoy it as is, or add your preferred sweeteners or creamers to taste.
9. Sit back, relax, and savor the unique taste of Kona coffee!

By following these steps, you can enjoy a delicious cup of Kona coffee brewed to perfection.

Kona blend

Ingredients:

- Kona blend coffee beans
- Water

Instructions:

1. Grind the Kona blend coffee beans to a medium-coarse consistency, similar to sea salt.
2. Heat water to just below boiling, around 200°F (93°C).
3. Place the ground Kona blend coffee into a coffee maker or a pour-over filter.
4. Pour hot water over the coffee grounds, making sure to saturate them evenly. Use a ratio of about 1 to 2 tablespoons of coffee per 6 ounces of water, depending on your preferred strength.
5. Allow the coffee to steep for about 3-4 minutes for optimal flavor extraction.
6. After steeping, gently stir the coffee to mix the grounds.
7. If using a pour-over method, carefully remove the filter containing the grounds.
8. Pour the brewed Kona blend coffee into a mug and enjoy it as is, or add your preferred sweeteners or creamers to taste.
9. Sit back, relax, and savor the smooth and flavorful taste of Kona blend coffee!

While Kona blend coffee may not have the same depth and complexity as pure Kona coffee, it still offers a delicious and satisfying coffee experience.

Kona coffee rub

Ingredients:

- 1/4 cup finely ground Kona coffee beans
- 2 tablespoons brown sugar
- 1 tablespoon paprika
- 1 tablespoon garlic powder
- 1 tablespoon onion powder
- 1 tablespoon ground black pepper
- 1 teaspoon ground cumin
- 1 teaspoon chili powder
- 1 teaspoon salt

Instructions:

1. In a mixing bowl, combine the finely ground Kona coffee beans, brown sugar, paprika, garlic powder, onion powder, ground black pepper, cumin, chili powder, and salt.
2. Stir the ingredients together until well combined, ensuring that there are no lumps and that the spices are evenly distributed throughout the mixture.
3. Store the Kona coffee rub in an airtight container or jar until ready to use.
4. To use the rub, generously coat your choice of meat (such as steak, ribs, or pork chops) with the Kona coffee rub, pressing it into the meat to adhere.
5. Allow the meat to marinate with the rub for at least 30 minutes to an hour, or overnight in the refrigerator for maximum flavor infusion.
6. Grill, roast, or barbecue the meat as desired until it reaches your preferred level of doneness, ensuring that the rub forms a flavorful crust on the exterior.
7. Serve the meat hot off the grill or out of the oven, and enjoy the rich and aromatic flavors of the Kona coffee rub!

This Kona coffee rub adds depth and complexity to your favorite meats, creating a deliciously flavorful dish that's perfect for any occasion. Adjust the quantities of spices according to your taste preferences, and feel free to experiment with additional herbs and seasonings for a custom blend.

Kalbi ribs

Ingredients:

- 3 pounds beef short ribs, cut across the bone into thin strips (about 1/4 inch thick)
- 1/2 cup soy sauce
- 1/4 cup brown sugar
- 2 tablespoons sesame oil
- 4 cloves garlic, minced
- 1 tablespoon grated ginger
- 2 green onions, chopped
- 1 tablespoon sesame seeds (optional, for garnish)
- Thinly sliced green onions (optional, for garnish)

Instructions:

1. In a mixing bowl, combine the soy sauce, brown sugar, sesame oil, minced garlic, grated ginger, and chopped green onions to make the marinade.
2. Place the beef short ribs in a large resealable plastic bag or a shallow dish. Pour the marinade over the ribs, making sure they are evenly coated. Seal the bag or cover the dish and refrigerate for at least 4 hours, or overnight for best results.
3. Preheat your grill to medium-high heat.
4. Remove the ribs from the marinade, shaking off any excess, and discard the remaining marinade.
5. Grill the ribs for 3-4 minutes per side, or until they are cooked to your desired level of doneness and have nice grill marks.
6. Transfer the grilled Kalbi ribs to a serving platter and garnish with sesame seeds and thinly sliced green onions, if desired.
7. Serve the Kalbi ribs hot with steamed rice and your favorite side dishes, such as kimchi and pickled vegetables.

Enjoy the tender, flavorful Kalbi ribs with their deliciously caramelized exterior and juicy interior, perfect for a Korean barbecue feast at home!

Pineapple salsa

Ingredients:

- 2 cups fresh pineapple, diced
- 1/2 cup red bell pepper, diced
- 1/4 cup red onion, finely chopped
- 1 jalapeño pepper, seeded and minced (adjust to taste)
- 1/4 cup fresh cilantro, chopped
- Juice of 1 lime
- Salt, to taste

Instructions:

1. In a mixing bowl, combine the diced pineapple, red bell pepper, red onion, minced jalapeño pepper, and chopped cilantro.
2. Squeeze the lime juice over the mixture and toss gently to combine.
3. Season the pineapple salsa with salt to taste, adjusting the amount as needed.
4. Cover the bowl with plastic wrap and refrigerate the salsa for at least 30 minutes to allow the flavors to meld together.
5. Once chilled, give the pineapple salsa a final stir and taste, adjusting the seasoning if necessary.
6. Serve the pineapple salsa as a topping for grilled chicken, fish, or shrimp, or as a dip with tortilla chips. It's also delicious in tacos, salads, or alongside grilled meats.
7. Enjoy the sweet and tangy flavors of this homemade pineapple salsa as a vibrant and refreshing addition to your favorite dishes!

Feel free to customize this pineapple salsa recipe to suit your taste preferences by adding ingredients like diced tomatoes, diced avocado, or finely chopped red chili peppers for extra heat.

Mango salsa

Ingredients:

- 2 ripe mangoes, peeled, pitted, and diced
- 1/2 red bell pepper, diced
- 1/4 cup red onion, finely chopped
- 1 jalapeño pepper, seeded and minced (adjust to taste)
- 1/4 cup fresh cilantro, chopped
- Juice of 1 lime
- Salt, to taste

Instructions:

1. In a mixing bowl, combine the diced mangoes, red bell pepper, red onion, minced jalapeño pepper, and chopped cilantro.
2. Squeeze the lime juice over the mixture and toss gently to combine.
3. Season the mango salsa with salt to taste, adjusting the amount as needed.
4. Cover the bowl with plastic wrap and refrigerate the salsa for at least 30 minutes to allow the flavors to meld together.
5. Once chilled, give the mango salsa a final stir and taste, adjusting the seasoning if necessary.
6. Serve the mango salsa as a topping for grilled fish, chicken, or pork. It's also delicious served with tortilla chips as a dip, or as a topping for tacos, salads, or grilled seafood.
7. Enjoy the sweet and tangy flavors of this homemade mango salsa as a refreshing addition to your favorite dishes!

Feel free to customize this mango salsa recipe to suit your taste preferences by adding ingredients like diced tomatoes, diced avocado, or finely chopped red chili peppers for extra heat.

Pineapple coleslaw

Ingredients:

- 4 cups shredded cabbage (green or a mix of green and purple cabbage)
- 1 cup shredded carrots
- 1 cup diced pineapple (fresh or canned, drained)
- 1/4 cup chopped fresh cilantro
- 1/4 cup mayonnaise
- 2 tablespoons Greek yogurt (or sour cream)
- 2 tablespoons apple cider vinegar
- 1 tablespoon honey (optional, for added sweetness)
- Salt and black pepper, to taste

Instructions:

1. In a large mixing bowl, combine the shredded cabbage, shredded carrots, diced pineapple, and chopped fresh cilantro.
2. In a separate small bowl, whisk together the mayonnaise, Greek yogurt (or sour cream), apple cider vinegar, and honey (if using), until smooth and well combined.
3. Pour the dressing over the cabbage mixture and toss until the vegetables are evenly coated with the dressing.
4. Season the pineapple coleslaw with salt and black pepper to taste, adjusting the amount as needed.
5. Cover the bowl with plastic wrap and refrigerate the coleslaw for at least 30 minutes to allow the flavors to meld together.
6. Once chilled, give the pineapple coleslaw a final toss and taste, adjusting the seasoning if necessary.
7. Serve the pineapple coleslaw as a side dish or topping for sandwiches, burgers, tacos, or grilled meats. Enjoy its sweet and tangy flavors!

Feel free to customize this pineapple coleslaw recipe to suit your taste preferences by adding ingredients like chopped red onion, sliced bell peppers, or jalapeño peppers for extra heat. You can also adjust the amount of mayonnaise and Greek yogurt (or sour cream) to achieve your desired creaminess level.

Taro chips

Ingredients:

- 1 large taro root
- Vegetable oil, for frying (if deep-frying)
- Salt, to taste

Instructions:

1. Peel the taro root and slice it thinly into rounds using a sharp knife or a mandoline slicer. Aim for slices that are about 1/8 inch thick for best results.
2. Place the taro slices in a large bowl of cold water and let them soak for about 10-15 minutes. This helps to remove excess starch from the taro, which can cause the chips to become soggy during frying.
3. Drain the taro slices and pat them dry thoroughly with paper towels to remove any excess moisture.
4. If deep-frying: Heat vegetable oil in a deep fryer or a large heavy-bottomed pot to 350°F (175°C). Carefully add the taro slices to the hot oil in batches, making sure not to overcrowd the pot. Fry the taro slices for 3-5 minutes, or until they are golden brown and crispy. Use a slotted spoon to transfer the fried taro chips to a paper towel-lined plate to drain excess oil. Repeat with the remaining taro slices.
5. If baking: Preheat your oven to 350°F (175°C). Place the taro slices in a single layer on a baking sheet lined with parchment paper. Lightly brush or spray the taro slices with vegetable oil and sprinkle with salt. Bake for 20-25 minutes, flipping the slices halfway through, until they are golden brown and crispy.
6. Once the taro chips are cooked, season them with salt to taste while they are still warm. Allow them to cool completely before serving.
7. Serve the taro chips as a crunchy snack on their own, or pair them with your favorite dip, such as salsa, guacamole, or hummus.

Enjoy the crispy and flavorful taro chips as a healthier alternative to store-bought potato chips!

Macadamia crusted

Ingredients:

- 4 boneless, skinless chicken breasts or fish fillets (such as mahi-mahi, tilapia, or salmon)
- 1 cup macadamia nuts, finely chopped or crushed
- 1/2 cup breadcrumbs (optional, for added texture)
- 1/4 cup all-purpose flour
- 2 eggs, beaten
- Salt and pepper, to taste
- Olive oil or cooking spray, for greasing

Instructions:

1. Preheat your oven to 375°F (190°C) and lightly grease a baking dish with olive oil or cooking spray.
2. If using chicken breasts, place them between two sheets of plastic wrap and gently pound them to an even thickness using a meat mallet or rolling pin. Season both sides of the chicken breasts or fish fillets with salt and pepper to taste.
3. Set up a breading station with three shallow dishes. Place the flour in the first dish, beaten eggs in the second dish, and chopped macadamia nuts (and breadcrumbs, if using) in the third dish.
4. Dredge each chicken breast or fish fillet in the flour, shaking off any excess. Dip it into the beaten eggs, allowing any excess to drip off. Then press the chicken or fish into the macadamia nut mixture, coating it evenly on all sides.
5. Place the coated chicken breasts or fish fillets in the prepared baking dish. If desired, you can drizzle a little olive oil over the top of each piece for added moisture and crispiness.
6. Bake in the preheated oven for 20-25 minutes, or until the chicken is cooked through (internal temperature of 165°F/75°C) or the fish flakes easily with a fork.
7. Once cooked, remove the macadamia-crusted chicken or fish from the oven and let it rest for a few minutes before serving.
8. Serve the macadamia-crusted chicken or fish hot with your favorite side dishes, such as rice, steamed vegetables, or a salad.

Enjoy the delicious combination of crunchy macadamia nuts and tender chicken or fish in this flavorful and satisfying dish!

Macadamia nut dressing

Ingredients:

- 1/2 cup macadamia nuts, toasted
- 1/4 cup olive oil
- 2 tablespoons white wine vinegar or apple cider vinegar
- 1 tablespoon honey or maple syrup
- 1 clove garlic, minced
- 1 tablespoon fresh lemon juice
- Salt and pepper, to taste
- Water, as needed to thin out the dressing

Instructions:

1. Start by toasting the macadamia nuts. Preheat your oven to 350°F (175°C). Spread the macadamia nuts in a single layer on a baking sheet and toast them in the preheated oven for 8-10 minutes, or until lightly golden and fragrant. Keep an eye on them to prevent burning. Once toasted, remove them from the oven and let them cool slightly.
2. In a blender or food processor, combine the toasted macadamia nuts, olive oil, white wine vinegar or apple cider vinegar, honey or maple syrup, minced garlic, and fresh lemon juice.
3. Blend the ingredients until smooth and creamy. If the dressing is too thick, you can add water, 1 tablespoon at a time, until you reach your desired consistency.
4. Taste the dressing and season with salt and pepper to taste. Adjust the sweetness or acidity by adding more honey or lemon juice, if desired.
5. Transfer the macadamia nut dressing to a jar or airtight container and store it in the refrigerator until ready to use. The flavors will meld together as it chills.
6. Shake or stir the dressing well before using. Drizzle it over salads, grilled vegetables, or use it as a sauce for grilled chicken, fish, or shrimp.
7. Enjoy the creamy and flavorful macadamia nut dressing as a delicious addition to your favorite dishes!

Feel free to customize this dressing by adding ingredients like fresh herbs (such as basil or cilantro) or spices (such as paprika or cayenne pepper) for extra flavor.

Macadamia nut pie

Ingredients:

For the pie crust:

- 1 1/4 cups all-purpose flour
- 1/2 teaspoon salt
- 1/2 cup (1 stick) unsalted butter, cold and cut into small pieces
- 2-4 tablespoons ice water

For the filling:

- 1 cup granulated sugar
- 3/4 cup light corn syrup
- 1/4 cup unsalted butter, melted
- 3 large eggs
- 1 teaspoon vanilla extract
- 1 1/2 cups chopped macadamia nuts

Instructions:

1. Preheat your oven to 350°F (175°C).
2. To make the pie crust, in a large mixing bowl, combine the all-purpose flour and salt. Add the cold, cubed butter to the flour mixture and use a pastry cutter or your fingers to work the butter into the flour until the mixture resembles coarse crumbs.
3. Gradually add the ice water, 1 tablespoon at a time, mixing until the dough comes together and forms a ball. Be careful not to overwork the dough.
4. Flatten the dough into a disk, wrap it in plastic wrap, and refrigerate for at least 30 minutes to chill.
5. Once chilled, roll out the dough on a lightly floured surface into a circle large enough to fit into a 9-inch pie dish. Carefully transfer the dough to the pie dish and trim any excess dough from the edges. Crimp the edges of the pie crust as desired.

6. In a medium mixing bowl, whisk together the granulated sugar, light corn syrup, melted butter, eggs, and vanilla extract until well combined.
7. Stir in the chopped macadamia nuts until evenly distributed.
8. Pour the macadamia nut filling into the prepared pie crust.
9. Place the pie dish on a baking sheet to catch any drips, and bake in the preheated oven for 50-60 minutes, or until the filling is set and the crust is golden brown.
10. If the edges of the pie crust start to brown too quickly, you can cover them with aluminum foil or a pie shield halfway through baking.
11. Once baked, remove the macadamia nut pie from the oven and let it cool completely on a wire rack before slicing and serving.
12. Serve slices of macadamia nut pie with whipped cream or vanilla ice cream, if desired.

Enjoy the indulgent and nutty flavor of homemade macadamia nut pie as a delightful dessert for any occasion!

Haupia pie

Ingredients:

For the crust:

- 1 1/4 cups all-purpose flour
- 1/2 teaspoon salt
- 1/2 cup (1 stick) unsalted butter, cold and cut into small pieces
- 2-4 tablespoons ice water

For the haupia filling:

- 1/2 cup granulated sugar
- 1/2 cup cornstarch
- 3 cups coconut milk
- 1/2 teaspoon vanilla extract

For topping:

- Whipped cream or toasted coconut flakes (optional)

Instructions:

1. Preheat your oven to 375°F (190°C).
2. To make the crust, in a large mixing bowl, combine the all-purpose flour and salt. Add the cold, cubed butter to the flour mixture and use a pastry cutter or your fingers to work the butter into the flour until the mixture resembles coarse crumbs.
3. Gradually add the ice water, 1 tablespoon at a time, mixing until the dough comes together and forms a ball. Be careful not to overwork the dough.
4. Flatten the dough into a disk, wrap it in plastic wrap, and refrigerate for at least 30 minutes to chill.
5. Once chilled, roll out the dough on a lightly floured surface into a circle large enough to fit into a 9-inch pie dish. Carefully transfer the dough to the pie dish and trim any excess dough from the edges. Crimp the edges of the pie crust as desired.

6. Use a fork to prick the bottom of the pie crust several times to prevent it from puffing up during baking. Bake the crust in the preheated oven for 12-15 minutes, or until lightly golden brown. Remove from the oven and let it cool completely.
7. To make the haupia filling, in a medium saucepan, whisk together the granulated sugar and cornstarch. Gradually whisk in the coconut milk until smooth.
8. Place the saucepan over medium heat and cook the mixture, stirring constantly, until it thickens and comes to a gentle boil, about 5-7 minutes.
9. Remove the saucepan from the heat and stir in the vanilla extract. Let the haupia filling cool for a few minutes.
10. Pour the haupia filling into the cooled pie crust and smooth the top with a spatula. Place the pie in the refrigerator to chill and set for at least 2-3 hours, or until firm.
11. Once the haupia pie is set, you can optionally top it with whipped cream or toasted coconut flakes before serving.
12. Slice the haupia pie into wedges and serve chilled. Enjoy this delicious Hawaiian dessert!

Feel free to customize your haupia pie by adding fresh fruit on top or incorporating other flavors such as chocolate or coffee into the filling.

Haupia cake

Ingredients:

For the cake:

- 2 cups all-purpose flour
- 1 1/2 teaspoons baking powder
- 1/2 teaspoon baking soda
- 1/4 teaspoon salt
- 1/2 cup (1 stick) unsalted butter, softened
- 1 cup granulated sugar
- 2 large eggs
- 1 teaspoon vanilla extract
- 1 cup coconut milk
- 1/2 cup shredded coconut (optional)

For the haupia filling:

- 1 (13.5 oz) can coconut milk
- 1/2 cup granulated sugar
- 1/4 cup cornstarch
- 1/4 cup water
- 1 teaspoon vanilla extract

For assembly:

- Whipped cream or coconut whipped cream
- Shredded coconut (optional)
- Fresh fruit (optional)

Instructions:

1. Preheat your oven to 350°F (175°C). Grease and flour two 9-inch round cake pans or line them with parchment paper.
2. In a medium bowl, whisk together the flour, baking powder, baking soda, and salt. Set aside.

3. In a large mixing bowl, cream together the softened butter and granulated sugar until light and fluffy. Add the eggs, one at a time, beating well after each addition. Stir in the vanilla extract.
4. Gradually add the dry ingredients to the wet ingredients, alternating with the coconut milk, beginning and ending with the dry ingredients. Mix until just combined. Fold in the shredded coconut, if using.
5. Divide the cake batter evenly between the prepared cake pans. Smooth the tops with a spatula.
6. Bake in the preheated oven for 25-30 minutes, or until a toothpick inserted into the center of the cakes comes out clean. Remove from the oven and let the cakes cool in the pans for 10 minutes before transferring them to wire racks to cool completely.
7. While the cakes are cooling, prepare the haupia filling. In a saucepan, combine the coconut milk and granulated sugar. In a small bowl, dissolve the cornstarch in the water, then add it to the coconut milk mixture.
8. Cook the mixture over medium heat, stirring constantly, until it thickens and comes to a gentle boil. Remove from heat and stir in the vanilla extract. Let the haupia pudding cool completely.
9. Once the cakes and haupia pudding are completely cooled, assemble the cake. Place one cake layer on a serving platter or cake stand. Spread a layer of haupia pudding over the cake layer.
10. Place the second cake layer on top of the haupia pudding. Spread whipped cream or coconut whipped cream over the top of the cake. If desired, sprinkle shredded coconut over the whipped cream and decorate with fresh fruit.
11. Chill the haupia cake in the refrigerator for at least 1 hour before serving to allow the flavors to meld together.
12. Slice and serve the haupia cake chilled. Enjoy the delicious tropical flavors of this Hawaiian dessert!

Feel free to customize your haupia cake by adding other fillings or toppings, such as sliced bananas or mangoes, to enhance the tropical flavor profile.

Lava flow cocktail

Ingredients:

- 1 1/2 oz light rum
- 1 oz coconut cream
- 2 oz pineapple juice
- 1/4 cup fresh or frozen strawberries
- 1 oz cream of coconut (optional)
- Crushed ice
- Pineapple wedge and/or strawberry for garnish

Instructions:

1. In a blender, combine the rum, coconut cream, and pineapple juice. Add the cream of coconut if you want a sweeter and creamier drink.
2. Blend the mixture until smooth.
3. In a separate blender or food processor, puree the strawberries until smooth. You can add a splash of pineapple juice to help with blending, if needed.
4. Fill a glass with crushed ice.
5. Pour the blended rum and coconut mixture into the glass, filling it about halfway.
6. Spoon the strawberry puree over the top of the drink, allowing it to flow down the sides and create a lava-like effect.
7. If desired, gently stir the strawberry puree into the drink slightly to create a marbled effect.
8. Garnish the glass with a pineapple wedge and/or a strawberry.
9. Serve immediately with a straw and enjoy your refreshing Lava Flow cocktail!

Feel free to adjust the ingredients and proportions to suit your taste preferences. You can also experiment with different types of rum or add other tropical fruits for a unique twist on this classic Hawaiian cocktail.

Mai Tai

Ingredients:

- 1 1/2 oz light rum
- 1 1/2 oz dark rum
- 1 oz lime juice (freshly squeezed)
- 1/2 oz orange liqueur (such as triple sec or Cointreau)
- 1/2 oz orgeat syrup
- 1/2 oz simple syrup
- Pineapple wedge, cherry, and/or mint sprig for garnish

Instructions:

1. Fill a shaker with ice cubes.
2. Add the light rum, dark rum, lime juice, orange liqueur, orgeat syrup, and simple syrup to the shaker.
3. Shake well until chilled.
4. Strain the mixture into an old-fashioned glass filled with crushed ice.
5. Garnish with a pineapple wedge, cherry, and/or mint sprig.
6. Serve immediately with a straw and enjoy your refreshing Mai Tai!

Note: The Mai Tai is a versatile cocktail, and the recipe can be adjusted to suit your taste preferences. Some variations include using different types of rum, adjusting the sweetness with more or less syrup, or adding a float of dark rum on top for a richer flavor profile. Experiment with different ingredients to find your perfect Mai Tai recipe!

Hawaiian sunset cocktail

Ingredients:

- 1 1/2 oz vodka
- 3 oz pineapple juice
- 1/2 oz grenadine
- Splash of orange juice
- Pineapple wedge and maraschino cherry for garnish

Instructions:

1. Fill a highball glass with ice cubes.
2. Pour the vodka and pineapple juice over the ice in the glass.
3. Add a splash of orange juice for extra flavor and color.
4. Slowly pour the grenadine into the glass. It will sink to the bottom and create a gradient effect, resembling a sunset.
5. Stir gently, if desired, to slightly mix the layers.
6. Garnish with a pineapple wedge and maraschino cherry.
7. Serve immediately with a straw and enjoy your Hawaiian Sunset cocktail!

Feel free to adjust the ingredients and proportions to suit your taste preferences. You can also experiment with different garnishes or add a splash of soda water for a lighter version of this tropical drink.

www.ingramcontent.com/pod-product-compliance
Lightning Source LLC
LaVergne TN
LVHW081614060526
838201LV00054B/2252